Cats

by Jack Long

Table Of Contents

Introduction

"Even a cat can look at a king."
Lewis Carroll

Cats are comfort-loving creatures. They will take endless trouble to find the right place in which to snooze on a sunny day and then stretch out luxuriously in the sun. They naturally seek comfort and safety. In the evening a cat will often jump onto your warm lap, purring contentedly, and invite you to stroke it behind the ears or under the chin.

For generations cats have been associated with royalty. Sometimes they have been considered royalty themselves. The royal cats of Egypt and Siam roamed palaces and temples alike. In Egypt they were considered sacred and at one time they were worshipped. An Egyptian who harmed a cat was punished. Killing a cat was a crime and if the accused was found guilty, he was killed. The owner of a cat that died shaved off his or her eyebrows as a symbol of mourning. Costly spices were bought for the embalming process of the pet and a cat mummy was created for the body of the deceased. The burial ceremony was elaborate.

Legend has it that Siamese cats were pets of the royal princesses of Siam, were accorded all the privileges of the royal family, and often were bejeweled.

In early Rome the cat was considered a symbol of liberty. Libertas, the Roman goddess of Liberty, was usually depicted with regal cats lying at her feet.

Louis XV had a pet white Persian cat that has gone down in history. Some of his courtiers doused the cat with perfume and were angrily denounced by the king.

Before the time of Louis XV, however, the cat had gone through a bad period in history. During the Middle Ages the cat was not only mistrusted but was accused of being an associate of the devil and witches. In the 1400's Pope Innocent VIII decreed that all cats belonging to witches should be burned with their owners. No doubt this reaction had come about as church leaders worked hard to establish Christianity among pagan peoples, many of whom had revered the cat. And so fanatic cat haters made life miserable for an animal that a few generations before had enjoyed a superior status. For many years the poor cat was tortured, accused of evil actions, and often destroyed.

But the cat survived. Here is evidence of its resourcefulness, cunning, and its ability to fend for itself.

Even during the darkest days for the breed there were always individuals who defied civil and church authority and kept cats as pets, even though they might be accused of being in league with the devil. The cat's usefulness was an important factor in regaining acceptance; it was a great hunter of rats and mice.

In the early 1400's, during the dreadful days of Bubonic Plague, also known as the Black Death, it was noted that people living in areas that were relatively free of rats and mice were less likely to succumb to the plague. The popularity of the cat was on the rise!

It is also true that people were becoming more humane and considerate of animals in general. Particularly, their concern for those animals that proved helpful to them became greater!

By the early sixteenth century cats were once more largely accepted. It is true there will always be cat haters as opposed to cat lovers, and not many in-betweeners. Cats incite revulsion among some just as they inspire affection among others. And, of course, there are those who are physically allergic to cats. However, the cat comeback was officially established in 1871 when the very first, and very fancy, cat show was held at the Crystal Palace in London. The public attended in droves and the show was considered a great success. Since then cat shows have become increasingly popular and well publicized. Most large cities have cat clubs and they sponsor cat shows that are held annually. Cats are judged by standards which have been established by accredited cat associations. In the United States cat shows have been held since the 1870's. In 1895 a New York City cat show, and later in 1900, a cat show in Chicago marked an official beginning of interest in cat breeding.

Artists and writers have always found the cat appealing and they have done much to make people aware of the beauty, the grace, and the mystery of the cat.

No one knows who the first artist was to draw the picture of a cat or to fashion it as a piece of sculpture. Since ancient times, however, the cat has inhabited the art world. It stands to reason, and there is visual evidence as well, that the Egyptians were among the first cat artists. Much later, in A.D. 1100, a Chinese artist painted the "Brown and White Cat" that has become renowned. Moronbu, a Japanese artist, is noted for his woodcuts of cats which were published in Japan in 1683.

During the Renaissance in Europe outstanding artists often painted the Holy Family and the canvases usually included cats both regal and angelic. One of the most famous cat paintings of a later date is Renoir's "Woman with Cat" which he painted in 1875.

Literature has provided us with cats galore from Dick Whittington's cat to the cats of T.S. Eliot that eventually inspired the extremely successful and long-running musical, "Cats."

Many children have read and loved Dr. Seuss' *Cat in the Hat* along with Elizabeth Coatsworth's famous books include *The Cat Who Went to Heaven* and Don Marquis immortalized the alley cat when he wrote of Mehitabel and her friend Archy, the cockroach. Undoubtedly one of the best known cats in all of literature is Lewis Carroll's Cheshire cat who smiled so famously at Alice and then disappeared.

The appeal of cats is due not only to their beauty but also to their independence. Cat owners often find themselves in the position of trying to please their cats, rather than vice versa, as in the case with other pets.

The pages that follow will tell you more about the characteristics of the cat. A 'cat profile' will discuss the outstanding physical aspects of the cat. There will be a section on the care of the cat that is so vital to its health and well-being. The various breeds of cats will also be described and throughout there will be a portrait gallery to emphasize the extraordinary charm, self-sufficiency, and variety of a pet that grows increasingly popular.

About Cats

*". . . A very fine cat, a
very fine cat indeed."*
from *Boswell's Life of Johnson*

All Cats are classified into two groups: Shorthairs and longhairs. It doesn't take an expert, usually, to decide in which group a cat belongs. The most popular and largest group is the domestic shorthair, often referred to as a tabby. The stripped tabby is the earliest type of domestic cat known. It is believed by most authorities that these cats descended from the African Wildcat. Most of them are of medium size. Their bodies are slender but muscular. The average adult cat weighs from eight to nine pounds. Pampered pets can far exceed this weight. Most house cats are exceedingly easy-going, friendly in a rather remote way, and home-loving. Cats are usually very even tempered. It is too time consuming and too much trouble to be provoked and angry. If a cat is weary of your attention or disinterested, it simply walks away.

Shorthaired and long haired cats both appear in solid colors. White, black, and gray are the most often seen. The striped baby is the most prevalent. The word 'tabby' comes from the French 'tabis' which is a silk taffeta cloth. Striped tabbies are sometimes called tiger cats. Usually they have gray bodies with darker vertical stripes. Other colors inspire other names, such as the silver tabby or the red tabby, A cat with colored patches on its body is often refered to by cat fanciers as a blotched tabby. There are many color combinations. These cats are also known, if the basic color is white, as calico cats.

Close in appearance to the calico cat is the relatively rare tortoiseshell cat which has black, cream and orange swirls of various patterns on its body. Although the reason is not known, most calico and tortoiseshell cats are female. It is rare that a male cat with these color swirls is able to reproduce.

White spots on the throats of solid-colored cats are known as "lockets" or "buttons."

Here are some other color types:

1. Chinchilla — Silver-colored.
2. Maltese — Often called "blue" cats. Maltese refers to the color of the cat and is not a breed.
3. Whites — White cats have pink noses. Often their eyes are different colors—one yellow and one blue. If both eyes are blue, the cat is usually deaf.
4. Blacks — A true black cat is jet black from the end of its tail to the tip of its nose.
5. Smoke-colored cats — These cats have hair that is white at the base and black at the tips.
6. Ginger or Marmalades — Cats of this color range from pale orange to a deep, reddish orange.

Entire books have been written about the characteristics of cats. One of the most outstanding traits is independence. A certain stubborness is a part of this characteristic. It is almost impossible to make a cat do something that it does not want to do. The well-trained dog comes when called. No matter how well-trained a cat is, it "decides" whether or not it will appear when it is summoned.

Cats have excellent memories. They remember people who have treated them kindly and they do not forget those who may have been cruel to them.

It has often been said that cats become more attached to places then they do to people, and there is little proof to the contrary. Many stories have been recounted of families who moved with their cat to a new locale some distance away. The cat disappears and much later turns up at the old homeplace. While these stories may be exaggerated from time to time, there is no doubt but that cats have favorite chairs and favorite spots. There is a bit of a paradox here since cats are among the best traveled pets of all. Ship cats have sailed the seven seas and via shipboard have migrated from country to country.

In addition to house cats and ship cats, there are warehouse cats and store cats. For many a cat the farm is home with the barn as headquarters.

There are many common sayings about the cat, usually based on observing some characteristic of the animal. Among them:

"Curiosity killed a cat." Applied to a person, this suggests that if you are too curious you may get into trouble.

"Honest as a cat when the cream is out of reach." Obviously suggesting someone who cannot be trusted.

"When the cat's away, the mice will play." Sometimes when the employer is not present, the employee takes advantage.

"Be made a cat's paw." To be the puppet or pawn of someone else.

"The cat has his tongue." To lack words to express one's self or to be speechless.

Scientific classification places the cat in the order Carnivora. The cat's family is Felidae, and the genus is Felis. (Remember Felix, the cat, who preceded Garfield of the comics!) The domestic cat of all breeds is genus Felis, species catus. This is sometimes stated as F. Domesticus.

In scientific terms or just in common terms, the cat is a comfort, a companion, and a joy for old and young alike.

It has been estimated that cats spend up to two-thirds of their lives sleeping, and the position of the animal depends very much on the temperature around it.

Cat Profile

*"The fog comes
on little cat feet."*
Carl Sandburg

When Sandburg compared the fog to the feet of a cat, he was, of course, thinking of how silently a cat gets about. This is an art that has stood the animal in good stead as a hunter. It is an ability that can be rather unsettling when a cat is suddenly by your side with no advance warning whatsoever.

Cats' paws are soft and padded. Compared to other animals their feet are rather tender. The front paws of a cat each have five toes, all equipped with extremely sharp claws that can be sheathed or extended. The bared claw is an effective weapon, a tool for eating, and an excellent aid in climbing. As a hunter, a cat first stuns and then captures its victim with a blow of the paw.

Cats usually have thirty teeth, although some cats have thirty-two.

In the front of the mouth are the incisors, or cutting teeth, which are the smallest. The premolars and the molars in the back of the mouth are for grinding and chewing of their food. The sharp canines, or eyeteeth, are used to seize and tear their food into bite-sized pieces. Cats usually lose some of their teeth as they grow older.

To most people a cat's eyes are the outstanding feature. The standard eye colors are amber, blue, yellow, and green. A cat's steady gaze can be both intriguing and disconcerting. The iris, or the colored circle, is most easily identified from breed to breed and from cat to cat. Again, it is the iris of th eye that is among the most distinctive features of the cat. When confronted with bright light or during the sunniest part of the day, the iris contracts, or squeezes together, thus

shutting out much of the glare. In a dim light, or at night, the iris opens much wider than it does in the eyes of other animals. This allows the cat to see much better than most animals when there is little light. Contrary to popular belief, however, a cat is unable to see in total darkness. It should also be noted that cats are color-blind.

Everyone is aware how a cat's eyes will glow in a dim light or in the dark. The cat has a built-in reflecting mechanism that enables it to see better in such a situation. This built-in mechanism is really a layer of cells forming a large part of the inner eye. It is called 'tapetum' and is pink, gold, blue, or green, reflecting different colors as the light changes.

As already noted, a cat's coat is either long-haired or short-haired. It is usually soft and silky. A sleek, glossy coat indicates a healthy cat. The whiskers of a cat are attached to nerves in the skin. Originally, it was thought that a cat never entered an opening that was less wide than its whiskers. This is not true. The whiskers are not used for measuring space. They are used rather more like radar to keep a cat from bumping into objects or to help it to feel its way through bushes.

The cat's swiftness, coordination, and incredible sense of balance enables it to avoid or escape many dangerous situations. Nature has designed a creature that can move with agility, speed, and, if necessary, with caution.

It is a splendid animal to watch in motion and to observe in repose.

Cat Care

"A harmless, necessary cat . . ."
Shakespeare

Granted, if you are a cat person, then having a cat is 'necessary,' but 'harmless' is a two-way street. The cat should not be threatened with any preventable affliction, (therefore of no harm to itself) and a cat free of problems is definitely 'harmless' when it comes to worrying on the part of the concerned owner. Cat care is of utmost importance.

To begin with, the cat is most helpful in taking care of itself. The mother cat—one of the best mothers in the animal kingdom—not only does a splendid preliminary job in caring for her kittens, but instills in them basic procedures for taking care of themselves. The innate intelligence of the cat is also an important factor. Some might term it 'cat sense.' The animal has a great instinct for self-preservation. It has a set of safety rules that seem to be inbred. The old saying, "Fools rush in where angels fear to tread," if adapted to cat territory might be stated, "Dogs rush in where cats fear to tread." Certainly, cats are more suspicious and hesitant creatures. They beat a hasty retreat if danger seems imminent. But all cats, if they are to attain the ultimate in care, can do with a considerable amount of outside help.

Here are some hints on cat care for the owner: Discipline is a word that really doesn't apply to cats in the strictest sense, but there is often the need to try to correct behavior. If a cat does something that needs to be discouraged, shake your finger close to its face and say, "No!" in a strong firm voice. If the offense is about to recur, repeat the "No" as deep a voice as possible. An aid to your remonstrance is oil of citronella, available in drug stores. All cats dislike the smell of it intensely so sprinkling a very few drops of it on the disputed territory, such as furniture or other areas, should end the problem.

In a more serious vein there are ailments and diseases for which the cat owner should always be on the alert. Cats can be victims of several kinds of disease problems. These include: (1) deficiency diseases, (2) infectious diseases, (3) parasitic diseases, and (4) problems (usually accidents) that may need special treatment, even surgery.

Deficiency diseases: The lack of vitamins A and D is a frequent problem, particularly in the case of the young adult cat. Liver and fish are rich sources of these vitamins and should be included in the diet. Feeding raw meat two or three times a week corrects pellagra which is caused by a lack of nicotinic acid. Anemia and rickets, both rare for a well-fed cat, are also deficiency diseases caused by a lack of vitamin D.

Infectious diseases: Feline Infectious Enteritis is the most dangerous disease for a cat. Not only is it extremely contagious, it is a killer. Fortunately, vaccination is a sure preventive. The new cat owner should have the cat inoculated immediately. The veterinarian will also inform you as to a schedule of booster shots. Cats can contact many human ailments, such

Cats seem to spend an inordinate amount of time performing their daily ablutions, but, although they wash themselves very thoroughly, it is an often neglected fact that many cats still need regular grooming. Longhaired varieties in particular (like this beautiful white Longhair, left) need a daily brushing and combing program by their owners so that loose hairs can be removed. This will stop the hair from matting uncomfortably and will also prevent the cat from swallowing hairs which could form a hairball in the stomach. If groomed carefully from an early age, the cat will learn to accept and welcome it as part of its normal routine.

as bronchitis, the common cold, and even pneumonia. Whooping cough is another disease to which they are susceptible. Ailing human beings with these diseases should not play with cats, even when convalescing.

Parasitic diseases: If a cat spends anytime outdoors, it is most likely to have fleas. Not only are fleas an aggravation, they can also infect a cat with other parasites such as tapeworms or hookworms. Insecticides especially prepared for cats are readily available. Read the instructions carefully. If the cat scratches its ears frequently or shakes its head violently, it probably has ear mites. Check with your veterinarian, but it is comforting to know that this condition is also easily remedied.

Special problems: Unfortunately it is not true that a cat always lands on its feet. Accidents, especially from falls, can and do happen. Also, bones ingested with food may produce alarming symptoms. Cystic ovaries, indicated by marked nervous symptoms, requires surgical correction. The prompt attention of a veterinarian is vital in all of these cases.

Any cat owner is faced with the decision whether or not to have the cat neutered (if male) or spayed (if a female). Unless one intends to breed cats, this procedure is always recommended. The cat population, forever on the increase, dictates this action.

Diet for cats is not difficult if common sense is followed. Cats are natural meat eaters. Canned cat foods on the market are good but should not be relied on exclusively. Dry cat foods should be introduced for variety. Raw liver, in moderation, is always a treat, as is cooked chicken and fish, carefully boned. Some cats like milk; others don't. For some cats too much milk means diarrhea. One observes and acts accordingly.

Don't feel that your cat is ailing if you see it eating grass. This is a necessary part of a cat's diet as it is a definite aid to the digestion. If the cat does not have access to the out-of-doors, it is advisable to provide grass by growing it in a box or pot.

The average cat will consent to one meal a day and prefers it in the evening.

The concerned cat owner equips the pet with a collar and a name tag. All collars should have an elastic insert. This allows the cat to slip out of the collar in case it gets caught on some obstruction.

There are many responsibilities connected with owning a cat, but they all are labors of love when they result in a healthy, contented pet.

Cat Communication

"Can't we talk this over?"
Anonymous

Side by side, the two cats at the left appear to be in close communication. Body language is an important part of a cat's vocabulary. The twitching of a tail can speak volumes.

All cats have an extensive vocabulary. Some of the "words" are easily heard. Other expressions are interpreted through observance. Owner and pet develop a repertory of understanding. The vocal words are usually associated with hunger — "Please, feed me now," or the need or desire to go outside, "Please let me out!" There are cats who "speak" loudly and cats with very soft miaows, but the demands are always quite clear.

Sometimes actions speak louder than words. A cat can sit by the door and fix its owner with a penetrating stare that demands action. It can flatten its ears when angry, and rub against you to remind you that it is chow time, or just time to show affection.

Purring, of course, is a soft but rapid-fire communication expressing contentment. Claws can also be used as parts of speech. A contented cat on a warm lap will dig in its claws if there is an indication that it is about to be unseated. An irritable or angry cat also "speaks" with its claws!

Cat conversation with another cat is sometimes conducted by nose and even by whiskers. Body contact can be gentle and affectionate. There is also a great range of vocal language: hisses and growls if the cat is threatened, and discordant "songs" if the cat is feeling romantic. Mother cats have a special language for their kittens, including warning miaows and time-for-dinner sounds.

Siamese cats are surely the most vocal of all cats and depend on their human associates more than other cats do. Their loud, mournful utterances demand attention.

Cat language is direct and easily understood. The wise owner lends an immediate ear and pays close attention to what the cat is saying.

Domestic Shorthair: This group represents the majority of cats. They are able to take care of themselves under almost any condition. The breed appears in a greater variety of sizes than any other.

Burmese: These cats arrived in the United States from Burma in 1930. They are similar to the Siamese. Burmese have a coat that is solid seal-brown. Sometimes it shades to almost a tan on the chest and underbody. Their eyes are a brilliant golden yellow.

Abyssinian: Supposedly these cats originated in ancient Egypt where they have been bred and raised for centuries. They are usually soft-voiced, and are particularly popular in England. They have green, yellow, or hazel eyes. Coat coloring is varied but it is most often reddish or dark brown.

Manx: This is a strange-looking breed with a very short tail or no tail at all. Legend claims that Noah shut the door of the ark just as the cat was entering, and so we have the tailless Manx. These cats originally lived on the Isle of Man, in the Irish Sea.

Russian Blue: A breed with short, thick fur and bright green eyes. It is a large cat and is sometimes referred to as "the king of the short-haired cats."

Rex: This breed is noted for its soft, curly coat. Even its whiskers are curly. The breed was developed in Great Britain.

Siamese: The two most usual color types are seal-point and blue-point. The seal-point is most common. It has a lightly colored body. The darker ears, face, feet, and tail are called "points." Various color types include chocolate-point, lilac-point, and red-point. Sometimes the eyes of a Siamese are slightly crossed. These royal cats of Siam were once palace and temple cats in that country. They first appeared in the Western Hemisphere in the 1880's.

Birman: According to legend this breed once watched over the temples of Burma where they were considered sacred cats. Their leader was supposedly the reincarnation of an abbott and the golden shading in the coat of the Birman is a reflection of the halo that shone above the abbott's head. It is a longhair cat.

Calling All Cats

*"What immortal hand or eye
Could frame thy fearful symmetry."*
William Blake

When Blake wrote the lines above, he was referring to the tiger, a member of the same family as our domestic cat. The family resemblance is evidenced in the picture of the cat on the left. One can easily visualize a tiger in the same position, bending low to drink from a jungle river.

The domestic cat, however, comes in many more models and patterns than its "cousin," the tiger. There are about thirty different recognized cat breeds. Here are some of the best known.

Longhairs: This breed is often called Persian and makes up one of the largest of the pedigree groups. (Of course, many nonpedigree cats have long hair.) Originally the longhair group resulted from the interbreeding of Persian and Angora cats. The Blue Persian is often called "the patrician of the cat shows." A good Longhaired white is considered by many the example of a perfect cat. In general Longhairs follow the same color patterns as Domestic Shorthairs.

Rare Breeds: These include Australian cats thought to be a variation of the Siamese breed. Tibetan Temple Cats are seldom seen outside China. Other rare types are Paraguayan, Japanese Kimona, Malay cat, Oriental Bobtailed, Maine Coon Cat, and Maltese. A postscript on the Domestsic Shorthair and nonpedigree tabby cat: They are said to be the most tiger-like of all the cats as they retain more of the typical wild-cat markings. The typical tabby markings are a large "M" on the forehead, two "chains" of darker fur around the neck, and identical "butterfly" marks on the shoulders. A popular myth is that the prophet Mohammed bent to stroke a tabby cat and left his initial on the cat's head for posterity.

All types of Siamese are blue-eyed, affectionate, and highly intelligent. Unlike most cats, however, they are fairly demanding of your time and attention.
Right: White long-haired kitten.

Cats on Camera

"Watch the birdie!"
Anonymous

In Britain many people consider it lucky to see a black cat cross their path, while in the United States and elsewhere the black cat is a symbol of bad luck!

Since the Egyptians first domesti-
cated cats over 3,000 years ago, to
act as rodent catchers in their grain
stores, people have been trying to
impose their wills on the cat. Breed-
ers thought they had successfully
managed to breed the kink out of
the end of the Siamese's tail, but
this still recurs from time to time!

It is not difficult to obtain a fairly passable snapshot of the family cat, but when it comes to providing high quality color photographs that will be suitable for commercial purposes then it is a very different story. Cats cannot be trained to cooperate with the requirements of the photographer and, as is so often the case in our relationship with cats, humans may end up adapting their wishes to the capriciousness of the cat. However, with time and patience one can come up with some outstanding camera work. Witness for instance, the cat-food commercials often seen on television.

In their wild state cats are hunters and consequently do not easily make friends with other animals. However, one of the many anomalies concerning cats is that they can also be loving companions to other types of animals, as well as human beings. We have all seen cats curled up with puppies, or baby rabbits, or even on apparently friendly terms with the family canary! But, after thousands of years of so-called domestication, any cat owner will tell you that cats are never predictable.

The cat in the 'farewell' picture right) might be thinking, "Come back soon. I'll be waiting."

Published in the United States by .
Joshua Morris Publishing, Inc.
167 Old Post Road
Southport, Connecticut 06490